What is phonics?

Phonics helps children learn to read and write by teaching them the letter sounds (known as phonemes), rather than the letter names, e.g. the sound that 'c' makes rather than its alphabetic name. They then learn how to blend the sounds: the process of saying the sounds in a word or 'sounding out' and then blending them together to make the word, for example c – a – t = cat. Once the phonemes and the skill of blending are learnt, children can tackle reading any phonetically decodable word they come across, even ones they don't know, with confidence and success.

However, there are of course many words in the English language that aren't phonetically decodable, e.g. if a child gets stuck on 'the' it doesn't help if they sound it out and blend it. We call these 'tricky words' and they are just taught as words that are so 'tricky' that children have to learn to recognise them by sight.

How do phonic readers work?

Phonic reading books are written especially for children who are beginning to learn phonics at nursery or school, and support any programme being used by providing plenty of practice as children develop the skills of decoding and blending. By targeting specific phonemes and tricky words, increasing in difficulty, they ensure systematic progression with reading.

Because phonic readers are primarily decodable – aside from the target tricky words which need to be learnt, children should be able to read the books with real assurance and accomplishment.

Big Cat phonic readers:
Pet Cat, Big Cat

In Big Cat phonic readers the specific phonemes and tricky words being focussed on are highlighted here in these notes, so that you can be clear about what your child's learning and what they need to practise.

While reading at home together, there are all sorts of fun additional games you can play to help your child practise those phonemes and tricky words, which can be a nice way to familiarise yourselves with them before reading, or remind you of them after you've finished. In *Pet Cat, Big Cat*, for example:

- the focus phonemes are i (sit), c (cat), h (hunt), l (lot). Why not write them down and encourage your child to practise saying the sounds as you point to them in a random order. This is called 'Speed Sounds' and as you get faster and faster with your pointing, it encourages your child to say them as quickly as possible. You can try reversing the roles, so that you have a practice too!

- the tricky words are 'I', 'a' and 'the'. You can play 'Hide and Seek' by asking your child to close their eyes and count to 10, while you write each word on a piece of paper, hiding them somewhere in the room you're in or the garden for your child to find. As they find each one, they should try reading and spelling the word out.

Reading together

- Why not start by looking at the front cover of *Pet Cat, Big Cat* and talking about what you can see.

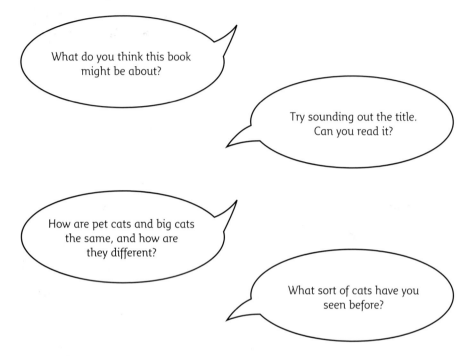

What do you think this book might be about?

Try sounding out the title. Can you read it?

How are pet cats and big cats the same, and how are they different?

What sort of cats have you seen before?

- Enjoy reading *Pet Cat, Big Cat* together, noticing the focus phonemes (i, c, h, l) and tricky words (I, a, the). It's useful to point to each word as your child reads, and encouraging to give them lots of praise as they go.

- If your child gets stuck on a word, and it's phonetically decodable, encourage them to sound it out. You can practise blending by saying the sounds aloud a few times, getting quicker and quicker. If they still can't read it, tell them the word and move on.

Talking about the book

- Use the pictures on pp18–19 to talk about what you know about pet cats and big cats, and what they do.

- Practise the focus phonemes from *Pet Cat, Big Cat* by asking your child to tell you the sound that, for example, the word 'hunt' begins with, and find specific words with the 'i' phoneme, for example, 'spit'.

Pet Cat, Big Cat

Written by Alison Hawes

Collins

I am a cat. I am a pet.

I can run and jump.

I sit in the sun a lot.

I hiss and spit if I am cross.

I hunt in the grass.

I drink milk. I lap it up.

I am a big cat. I am not a pet.

I can run fast.

I sit in the sun a lot.

I hiss and spit if I am cross.

I hunt in the grass.

I jump in the pond if it is hot.

Pet cats

Big cats

Getting creative

- Have some fun with your child by playing a game of 'I spy' using the focus phonemes from the book.

- You could play a game of 'Pairs' together to practise the tricky words from *Pet Cat, Big Cat*, where you write down 2 or 3 copies of each of the tricky words on separate pieces of paper, then muddle them up and place them all face down on the table, taking it in turns to try and find the pairs.

- If your child's enjoyed reading *Pet Cat, Big Cat* why not see if they'd like to draw a cat. Using the book for ideas, talk about what kind of cat they'd like to draw.

- They could then add a title to their drawing and some labels using their sounds to help them.

Other books at Level 1:

Fiction	Non-fiction
Sam and the Nut — Sheryl Webster, Giuditta Gaviraghi	Got It! — Charlotte Guillain, Lee Hasler Roberts
Ant and Snail — Paul Shipton, Jon Stuart	Pond Food — John Townsend, Pamela Anzalotti
We Are Not Fond of Rat! — Emma Chichester Clark	Pet Cat, Big Cat — Alison Hawes

Collins Big Cat
Reading Lions

Published by Collins
An imprint of HarperCollins*Publishers*
1 London Bridge Street
London
SE1 9GF

Author: Alison Hawes

Alison Hawes asserts her moral right to be identified as the author of this work.

British Library Cataloguing in Publication Data
A catalogue record for this publication is available from the British Library.

Designer: Sarah Elworthy
Parent notes authors: Sue Reed and Liz Webster

Acknowledgements
Photography: front cover, left: Alamy/Picture Partners; front cover, right: Corbis/Yann Arthus-Bertrand; back cover, 3: Alamy/Juniors Bildarchiv; 1, 10, 11, 15tr, 15br: Corbis/ Tom Brakefield; 1 (inset), 4, 14br: Alamy/Manor Photography; 2: Alamy/Gabe Palmer; 2 (inset), 5, 8, 14tr: Warren Photographic; 6, 14l: Alamy/Arco Images; 7: Corbis/Roy Morsch; 8 (inset), 15l: Corbis/Renee Lynn; 9, 13: Corbis/zefa/Theo Allofs; 12: Corbis/ Paul A. Souders

Printed and bound by RR Donnelley APS

www.collins.co.uk/parents